Every child learns to read in a different way and at his or her own speed. You can help your young reader improve and become more confident by encouraging his or her own interests and abilities. You can also guide your child's spiritual development by reading stories with biblical values and Bible stories, like I Can Read! books published by Zonderkidz. From books your child reads with you to the first books he or she reads alone, there are I Can Read! books for every stage of reading:

 SHARED READING
Basic language, word repetition, and whimsical illustrations, ideal for sharing with your emergent reader.

 BEGINNING READING
Short sentences, familiar words, and simple concepts for children eager to read on their own.

 READING WITH HELP
Engaging stories, longer sentences, and language play for developing readers.

 READING ALONE
Complex plots, challenging vocabulary, and high-interest topics for the independent reader.

 ADVANCED READING
Short paragraphs, chapters, and exciting themes for the perfect bridge to chapter books.

I Can Read! books have introduced children to the joy of reading since 1957. Featuring award-winning authors and illustrators and a fabulous cast of beloved characters, I Can Read! books set the standard for beginning readers.

A lifetime of discovery begins with the magical words **"I Can Read!"**

Visit www.icanread.com for information on enriching your child's reading experience.
Visit www.zonderkidz.com for more Zonderkidz I Can Read! titles.

Say with your mouth, "Jesus is Lord."
Believe in your heart that God raised him
from the dead. Then you will be saved.

Romans 10:9

ZONDERKIDZ

Paul Meets Jesus
Copyright © 2016 by Zondervan
Illustrations © 2016 by David Miles

Requests for information should be addressed to:
Zonderkidz, 3900 *Sparks Drive SE, Grand Rapids, Michigan 49546*

ISBN 978-0-31075076-5

Editor: Mary Hassinger
Art direction and design: Kris Nelson

Printed in China

15 16 17 18 19 20 /DHC/ 21 20 19 18 17 16 15 14 13 12 11 10 9 8 7 6 5 4 3 2 1

Adventure BIBLE

Paul Meets Jesus

Pictures by David Miles

ZONDERkidz

Saul was angry.

Not long ago,

a man named Jesus went all over the land

teaching about God.

Jesus told people

he was the Son of God.

Jesus was gone now,

but he still had many followers.

Saul did not like this.

Saul said, "The followers of Jesus
should be thrown in jail.

They are wrong.

Jesus is not the Son of God."

Saul did everything he could

to get Jesus' followers in trouble.

One day, Saul was walking

down the road.

He was on his way to a city

where followers of Jesus lived.

He wanted to arrest them.

A bright light flashed

from heaven!

Saul fell to the ground.

He was scared!

Saul heard a voice say,

"Saul, why are you trying to hurt me?"

Saul covered his head.

He asked, "Who are you?"

The voice said, "I am Jesus.

Now get up and go into the city.

You will be told what to do next."

There were some men

traveling with Saul.

They did not know what to say.

They heard the voice

but did not see anyone!

Saul got up.

When he opened his eyes,

he could not see anything!

He was blind!

His friends led him into the city.

Saul was blind for three days.

He did not eat or drink anything.

A man named Ananias lived in the city.

He loved Jesus.

One day, God spoke to Ananias
and said, "Find a man named Saul.
He is blind. Put your hands on him,
then he will be able to see."

Ananias was afraid.

He said, "God,

I have heard about Saul.

He is a bad man!

He tries to hurt Jesus' followers!"

But God said, "Go!

I chose this man.

I will use Saul to tell people

all over the world about me."

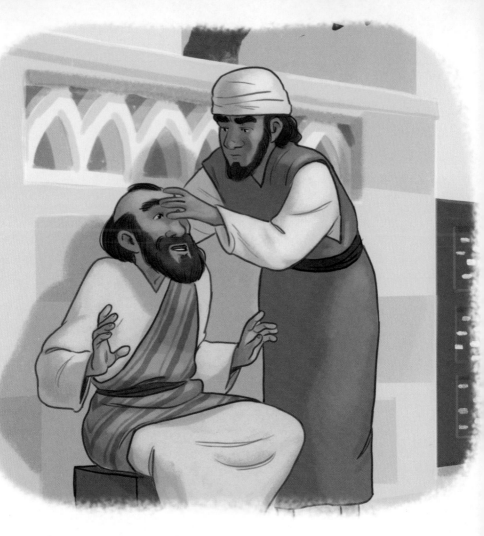

Ananias found Saul.

He placed his hands on Saul and said,

"Brother, Jesus has sent me

so that you may see again.

Be filled with the Holy Spirit."

Right away,

Saul could see again!

He got up,

and Ananias baptized him.

Saul was a new person.

He changed his name to Paul.

He believed that Jesus was God.

Paul began to teach about Jesus.
Everyone said, "Isn't this the man
who used to cause trouble
for Jesus' followers?"
But Paul didn't stop teaching.

Soon, Paul started to travel.

Sometimes he traveled with others,

and sometimes he went by himself.

Paul told everyone he met

the good news about Jesus.

In some places,

Paul was chased away.

But Paul did not give up.

In one city, there was a man

who could not walk.

He listened to every word Paul said.

Paul saw the lame man had faith.

Paul said, "Stand up!"

The man jumped up and began to walk.

The people were amazed.

Another time, Paul and his friend Silas
were thrown in jail.

God sent an earthquake.

The prison doors flew open!

Their chains fell off!

The jailer was so amazed

he asked Paul,

"What must I do to be saved?"

Paul also wrote letters.

He sent them to churches.

The letters told people

about the love of Jesus.

God changed Paul's life.

Paul became a good man.

Paul preached.

He helped many people.

Paul never stopped telling people
about the love of God.

People in Bible Times

Words to Live By:
And now these three remain: faith, hope and love.
But the greatest of these is love.
1 Corinthians 13:13

Saul/Paul

Saul was a Pharisee who hated Christians. After a miracle happened on his way to Damascus, and Jesus appeared to him, Saul became a Christian! He became a brave and powerful preacher and missionary. Paul wrote thirteen books of the Bible.

Did You Know

While Paul traveled all over the world preaching and teaching about Jesus, he did something wonderful for the believers—he prayed for them. Paul prayed for the Philippians and the Colossians and the people in Corinth. He prayed that these people, and the whole world, would grow to know and love Jesus. We can pray that same prayer for the people of the world.